SIMON & SCHUSTER BOOKS FOR YOUNG READERS
Simon & Schuster Building, Rockefeller Center
1230 Avenue of the Americas, New York, New York 10020
Copyright © 1983 by Jane Miller. First U.S. edition 1983. Originated by
J. M. Dent & Sons Ltd. First published in Great Britain in 1983. All rights
reserved including the right of reproduction in whole or in part in any form.
SIMON & SCHUSTER BOOKS FOR YOUNG READERS is a trademark of
Simon & Schuster.
Manufactured in the United States of America 10 9 8 7 6 5 4 3

Library of Congress Cataloging in Publication Data
Miller, Jane.   Summary: Introduces simple number concepts using color
photographs of favorite farm animals.   1. Counting—Juvenile literature.
[1. Counting.   2. Domestic animals—Pictorial works.]   I. Title.
OA113.M536   1983   513'.2   [E]   82-21622
ISBN: 0-671-66552-9

For Patricia Blake

Farm
Counting
Book

JANE MILLER

Simon & Schuster Books for Young Readers

Published by Simon & Schuster
New York · London · Toronto · Sydney · Tokyo · Singapore

1
one kitten

2
two lambs

3

three horses

4

four pigs

5

five cows

6

six dogs

7

seven ducks

8

eight swans

9

nine horseshoes

10
ten geese

Here is 1 puppy –

and 1 bed for the puppy.

How many cats are there?

Is there a bowl of milk for each cat?

Here are 3 cows.

1 donkey   1 foal   1 goat

3 animals altogether

How many ducks can you count?
How many white ducks are there?
Are there more white ducks than brown ducks?

How many piglets are there in this litter?

How many chicks are there in this brood?

How many geese can you see?

How many sheep are there?

How many ponies are there?

How many foals?

How many strawberries are there in this picture?

Are there the same number of strawberries in this picture?

Can you count how many eggs there are in this picture?

Following her highly successful "Farm Alphabet Book" –
hailed by "The Guardian" as 'a visual delight' – comes Jane
Miller's "Farm Counting Book", also illustrated with full-
colour photographs. Born and brought up in Australia,
Jane Miller started taking photographs at the age of ten,
and even at that age processed them herself. After living in
Thailand, India and the United States, she became a free-
lance photographer and began to work professionally.